Who

101 Questions and Answers That Every Christian Should Know, But Never Thought to Ask

By Thomas Shine

Golgotha Press
www.golgothapress.com

© 2011. All Rights Reserved.

Table of Contents

GOD'S BIGGEST BANG 6

HOW DID WE COME TO EXIST IF ADAM AND EVE ONLY HAD TWO SONS? 7
WAS THE WORLD REALLY CREATED IN SEVEN DAYS OR WAS THERE SOMETHING ELSE TO IT? 8
WHAT DOES IT MEAN WHEN THE BIBLE SAYS SOME WILL BE GIVEN DIFFERENT "REWARDS" IN HEAVEN? 8
WHY DID GOD COME TO EARTH TO DIE FOR OUR SINS? 9
HOW DID JESUS CHOOSE HIS DISCIPLES AND WHY? 9
WHY DID GOD CREATE FREE WILL? 10
HOW DID PEOPLE LIVE SO LONG IN GENESIS? 11

SEX, DRUGS AND ROCK'N'ROLL 12

IS DRINKING ALCOHOL SIN? 13
IS SMOKING OKAY? IS SMOKING CIGARS, CIGARETTES, OR MARIJUANA SIN? 14
WHAT IS WRONG WITH DRUGS--ISN'T ALCOHOL A DRUG? 15
THE BIBLE HAS PROSTITUTES AND SOME WERE EVEN HEROES; SO WHY IS PROSTITUTION WRONG? 15
IS HOMOSEXUALITY WRONG? 16
CAN A HOMOSEXUAL GO TO HEAVEN IF THEY HAVE A PERSONAL RELATIONSHIP WITH GOD? 17

MY MINISTER NEVER TOLD ME THAT 18

WHY IS THERE SUFFERING? 19
WHY IS THERE SUFFERING? 19
WHY DOES GOD EXIST? 20
WHY DO WE EXIST? 20
ARE WE TO TRULY TAKE THE BIBLE LITERALLY ALL THE TIME OR DOES IT EXAGGERATE AT TIMES? 21
CAN WE REALLY EAT ANYTHING WE DESIRE? 22
WHY ARE THERE FALSE TEACHERS? 22
HOW DO WE KNOW GOD EXISTS? 23
HOW DO WE KNOW JESUS WAS REAL? 23
HOW DID THE BIBLE COME INTO EXISTENCE? 24
WHO WROTE THE BIBLE? 25
HOW OLD IS THE BIBLE? 26

How was the Bible written? 27
Who created God? 27
Why would God let someone be mentally or
physically challenged? 28
What is speaking in tongues and how do you know if
someone is REALLY doing it? 29
Does God have a sense of humor? 30
What does it mean when it says Jesus was half God
and half man? Why couldn't he be all God? 32
What is the Trinity? 32
What does the Holy Spirit do? 33
Why aren't there prophets today like there were in
the Old Testament? 34
Would God really send a really good person to Hell?
What kind of God is that! 34
Where did idol worship come from? 35

WILL BUDDHA GO TO HEAVEN? 36

How did so many other religions come into existence
from two people? 37
Are Mormons and Jehovah Witnesses Christians? 38
Why are there so many sects of Christianity? (i.e.
Methodist, Baptist, Lutheran, etc) 39
Are Catholics Christian? 40
Will Jews who don't accept Christ go to Heaven? 41

NOT YOUR TYPICAL SUNDAY SCHOOL QUESTION .42

Are all Christians really Christians? 43
Some people in the Bible had multiple wives. Why can't
I? 44
Why are there so many languages spoken in the
world? 45
What is the correct language to read the Bible in and
why do some people think it can only be the King
James Version? 45
Should Christians be allowed to be wealthy? 46
How much is one supposed to tithe and what happens if
you do not? 47
Why do Jews not believe in Jesus; wasn't he the person
their prophets had been speaking of? 48

WHY IS ISRAEL THE HOLY LAND? 49
WHY IS THERE SO MUCH FIGHTING BETWEEN THE PEOPLE IN
THE HOLY LAND? 50
WHY DON'T WE PERFORM SACRIFICES ANYMORE? 51
IS IT WRONG TO KILL SOMEONE IN WAR? 52
ARE THERE ALIENS FROM OUTER SPACE? 53
ARE ANGELS REAL? 54
WILL CHRISTIANS WHO JUDGE OTHERS GO TO HEAVEN? 54
ARE DEMONS REAL? 55
WHY WOULD GOD LET A BABY HAVE AIDS? 56
IS ABORTION WRONG? 56
WHAT HAPPENS IF SOMEONE GREW UP IN A REMOTE REGION
THAT HAS NEVER HEARD OF GOD OR JESUS? WILL THEY GO TO
HELL? 57
IS SATAN ACTUALLY A FALLEN ANGEL OR JUST A GENERAL
NAME FOR A DEMON? 58
WHY DOESN'T GOD ANSWER MY PRAYERS? 59
THE DISCIPLES COULD PERFORM MIRACLES; WHY CAN'T
PEOPLE DO SO MORE TODAY? 59
JESUS SAID IF YOU HAVE FAITH YOU CAN MOVE A MOUNTAIN;
IF I CAN'T MOVE A MOUNTAIN DOES THAT MEAN I DON'T HAVE
FAITH? 60
WHAT IS GRACE AND MERCY? 61
WAS JONAH REALLY IN A WHALE? 62
WILL GIVING AWAY ALL MY POSSESSIONS MAKE ME A BETTER
CHRISTIAN? 63
WHY DID GOD MAKE SOME BODY PARTS THAT HAVE NO
PURPOSE (E.G., APPENDIX)? 63

DYING TO KNOW WHAT HAPPENS WHEN PEOPLE DIE 65

WOULD GOD REALLY LET SO MANY PEOPLE GO TO HELL? 66
WHEN WILL THE END OF THE WORLD TAKE PLACE? 66
WHY DO WE DIE? 67
WHAT HAPPENS WHEN WE DIE? 67
WHAT IS THE CORRECT WAY TO DISPOSE OF A BODY, BURIAL
ABOVE/BELOW GROUND OR CREMATE? 68
IF HEAVEN IS SO MUCH BETTER, WHY DO WE EVEN HAVE TO BE
ON EARTH? 70
WILL DOGS, CATS, AND ANIMALS GO TO HEAVEN? 70

WHAT WILL WE LOOK LIKE IN HEAVEN? 71

NOAH'S ARK 72

WHATEVER HAPPENED TO NOAH'S ARK IF IT DID EXIST?........73
WERE THERE DINOSAURS ON THE ARK? 73
HOW DID ALL THOSE ANIMALS FIT ON THE ARK?....................74
WHAT GOOD ARE MOSQUITOES FOR AND WHY WERE THEY PUT IN THE ARK? 75

WHOOPS, I SINNED AGAIN...76

WHY DO WE SIN WHEN WE KNOW WE SHOULD NOT?..............77
ARE ALL SINS FORGIVABLE? 77
WHAT HAPPENS IF A CHRISTIAN DOES SIN WHEN THEY KNOW THEY SHOULD NOT? 78
IS DIVORCE SIN?..79
IS IT SIN TO DIVORCE AND MARRY AGAIN?.............................80
IS SOME SIN OKAY WHILE OTHER SINS ARE NOT? 80
WHAT CONSTITUTES A SIN? WHAT IS RIGHT TO SOME IS WRONG TO OTHERS, SO WHAT MAKES A SIN AND WHO IS RIGHT? 81
IS SWEARING SIN? 81
IS WATCHING A R-RATED MOVIE SIN? 82
IS LOOKING AT PORNOGRAPHY SIN?..83
ARE STEALING AND KILLING REALLY EQUAL SINS? 83
IS IT SIN TO STEAL BREAD FOR A HUNGRY CHILD? 84
IF ANGER IS A SIN, WHY ARE WE ALLOWED THE EMOTION?....84
IF I'M SINGLE, WHY CAN'T I LUST AFTER ANOTHER PERSON IF I DON'T ACT OUT ON THAT LUST? NO HARM DONE, SO WHAT'S THE BIG DEAL? 85

BUYING MY WAY INTO HEAVEN?..................................87

IS BAPTISM A REQUIREMENT TO GO TO HEAVEN?....................88
WHAT HAPPENS WHEN A BABY OR YOUNG CHILD DIES BEFORE THEY HEAR ABOUT SALVATION? 88
DO YOU HAVE TO WORK FOR SALVATION?..............................89
WHAT HAPPENS TO THOSE THAT AREN'T CIRCUMCISED? 90
WHY WAS JESUS BAPTIZED?..90
WHY DID JESUS HAVE TO DIE; WHY COULDN'T GOD JUST FORGIVE? 91

God's Biggest Bang

How did we come to exist if Adam and Eve only had two sons?

Adam lived for 800 more years after he had his son Seth and he fathered other sons and daughters (Genesis 5:4). The ancient Jewish historian Josephus claimed that Adam had 33 sons and 23 daughters (F. Josephus, *The Complete Works of Josephus*, translated by W. Whiston, Kregel Publications, Grand Rapids, Michigan, 1981, 27).

Also, just because daughters were not mentioned prior to the story of Cain and Abel, it does not mean they did not have any sisters at that time. Often in the Bible, the focus is on the subject under discussion, and other facts lacking relevance to the subject are not even mentioned. Since we all came from Adam and Eve (Genesis 3:20; Acts 17:26), we must assume that in the beginning of mankind's population growth, God allowed for the marriage of brother and sister. It was not until the time of Moses that God prohibited this (Leviticus 18:9).

Though union with a close relative today will increase the probability of the child inheriting negative hereditary factors, in the early generations of mankind's population growth, we must assume that their gene pool was not as limited and restricted as they are today since they were much closer in ancestry to the perfect man and woman.

Was the world really created in seven days or was there something else to it?

This is a matter of much debate with some quoting the passages that claim a thousand years to God is like one day (Psalm 90:4; 2 Peter 3:8). Others quote Exodus 20:11 to insist they were literal days. There are a variety of inconclusive arguments such as one claiming that since the Bible tells us God spoke and it was done (Psalm 33:9) and things happened immediately when Jesus spoke, that this means that there was no delay in the creation. But this claim about immediate results when Jesus spoke was not always the case (Mark 11:12-14, 20-21), and even if it was, this is pure speculative reasoning. We simply cannot know for certain which position is the correct one, and either view is acceptable for a Christian.

What does it mean when the bible says some will be given different "rewards" in heaven?

Though the Bible is not clear about exactly what these rewards are, it may be because it is difficult to describe them to those who do not understand what heaven will really be like (1 Corinthians 2:9). Yet, there is a possible hint of some of these rewards in the discussion that Jesus had with the mother of John and James about who would sit on the sides of Jesus in his Kingdom, to which he replied that it would be given to those to whom the Father has chosen (Matthew 20:20-23).

Why did God come to earth to die for our sins?

Jesus came here to die for our sins because God the Father loves us (John 3:16) and does not want any of his creation to perish because of their sins (2 Peter 3:9; Ezekiel 18:32). Jesus chose to leave heaven in order to accomplish this in obedience to God the Father (Philippians 2:5-8).

How did Jesus choose his disciples and why?

Though the Bible does not clarify what caused him to specifically select those that he did, we do get some possible hints. Peter was a very religious man who had never eaten anything unclean in his entire life (Acts 10:14) and was obviously blessed by God the Father (Matthew 16:17). When seeing Nathanael, Jesus declared, "Behold an Israelite indeed, in whom is no guile!" (John 1:47). And Judas was selected even though Jesus knew he would betray him (John 6:64). Though we don't know the specific reason Jesus picked each disciple, we do know that God chooses the foolish, weak, despised, and base people of this world to confound the wise and the mighty (1 Corinthians 1:26-29).

Why did God create free will?

Though there is not any clear explanation in the Bible why God created free will, Justin Martyr believed that God allowed evil from the beginning of the creation because he wanted to give all of creation a free will to chose whether or not to follow God by their own choice. Justin explains, "But yet, since He knew that it would be good, He created both angels and men free to do that which is righteous, and He appointed periods of time during which He knew it would be good for them to have the exercise of free-will." (*Dialogue with Trypho* 102). These periods of time for mankind are probably a reference to our life here on earth.

How did people live so long in Genesis?

One of the things we notice is that most of the people who lived for a really long time were those who were born before the flood or those who were born in the centuries after the flood, with a general diminishing of the length of life as more generations passed to the point where even Abraham died before Noah's son Shem. It seems most probable that God allowed the lengthy lives to fulfill his original objective to populate the earth through procreation more rapidly (Genesis 1:28; Genesis 9:1).

Sex, Drugs and Rock'n'Roll

Is drinking alcohol sin?

The Bible does not consider drinking alcohol a sin. Even Jesus drank wine (1 Corinthians 11:25; Luke 7:34) and he speaks about drinking wine again in the coming kingdom of God (Mark 14:25). The first miracle of Jesus was turning six large containers of water into wine at a wedding where they had already been drinking (John 2:1-10). Alcohol was also used as a medicine (1 Timothy 5:23). The claims by some that all of these passages are talking about grape juice and that they were celebrating a wedding with grape juice is pure nonsense. Yet, the Bible does define alcohol abuse as sinful and warns that drunkards will not enter the kingdom of God (1 Corinthians 6:10; Galatians 5:21).

The priests in Old Testament times were not allowed to drink alcohol for the specific reason that could impair their ability to properly discern and teach (Leviticus 10:8-11), so the fact that Christians are now priests (Revelation 1:6) should be taken into consideration. In addition, we are not supposed to do anything to stumble our brothers. So, even if drinking alcohol in moderation is not sin, it can become sin if we drink in front of someone else who struggles with alcoholism (cf. Corinthians 8:9-13). Also, the apostle Paul instructs us, "And be not drunk with wine, wherein is excess; but be filled with the Spirit" (Ephesians 5:18).

Is smoking okay? Is smoking cigars, cigarettes, or marijuana sin?

Anything that is harmful to the body should be avoided because the body of a Christian is the temple of the Holy Spirit that dwells within (1 Corinthians 3:16, 6:19). There can be little doubt with today's research that tobacco cuts the lifespan of anyone who uses it and so to smoke tobacco is to destroy the temple of God, something Paul clearly identifies as forbidden (1 Corinthians 3:17). The same argument would apply to marijuana if it is determined to be harmful to your body.

In addition, since marijuana impairs judgment and makes one intoxicated, its abuse it similar to alcohol and would make that person subject to the same penalty of eternal death as the drunkard (1 Corinthians 6:10; Galatians 5:21). Even if marijuana were not harmful and it is not being abused by the user, its use by someone can still harm others with drug or alcohol problems (cf. Corinthians 8:9-13). And this passage would apply as well, "And be not drunk with wine, wherein is excess; but be filled with the Spirit" (Ephesians 5:18).

What is wrong with drugs--isn't alcohol a drug?

We cannot use the overall classifications of society such as "drugs" to determine biblical truth. Though alcohol and drugs may be similar in some ways, they are not the same thing in biblical text. Most mind-altering drugs today are harmful to the body and distort our ability to interface with God and to discern truth in our walk as Christians, even in small doses. When used simply for pleasure, we are making the decision to place ourselves in a spiritually weakened state and ignore the command in Scripture to avoid impairing ourselves (Ephesians 5:18). In biblical times, drug use was associated with sorcery (PHARMAKEIA IN THE GREEK, WHICH IS WHERE WE GET THE WORD PHARMACY) AND IDOLATRY and was condemned (Galatians 5:20; Revelation 9:21).

The Bible has prostitutes and some were even heroes; so why is prostitution wrong?

Though the prostitute Rahab became a biblical hero, it was because of her assistance to the people of God (Hebrews 11:31; James 2:25). This does not in any way condone her sins of prostitution. We are specifically told that prostitution is unlawful and unholy (Leviticus 19:29, 21:9; Deuteronomy 23:17; 1 Corinthians 6:15-16). And since any sexual activity outside of marriage is sin, this makes it quite certain that prostitution is also sin for both the prostitute and the one using the prostitute.

Is homosexuality wrong?

"Thou shalt not lie with mankind, as with womankind: it [is] abomination" (Leviticus 18:22; also cf. Leviticus 20:13, Romans 1:26-27). This passage is very clear and it cannot be explained away by clever attempts to manipulate it's meaning. There is a definite contrast being set up here with a comparison of homosexuality to a normal heterosexual relationship as established by God (Matthew 19:5-6). God identifies homosexuality as a sin and even calls it an abomination.

Can a homosexual go to heaven if they have a personal relationship with God?

A practicing homosexual will not go to heaven and is classified among other habitual sinners that will be cast into the Lake of Fire (1 Corinthians 6:9; 1 Timothy 1:10). Now, a homosexual who has given up on acting out this sin but still struggles with temptation is like any other Christian and will go to heaven. When the homosexual becomes a Christian, he becomes a new creature in Christ (2 Corinthians 5:17).

My Minister Never Told Me That

Why is there suffering?

Suffering is a result of the sin of Adam when he disobeyed God. Even death did not exist until that day (Genesis 2:17, 3:19). Once Adam sinned, the curses of sin fell upon mankind and the whole creation descended into a fallen state with death, sickness, sorrow, and pain (Genesis 3:15-19; also cf. Romans 5:12). We now wait for the day when suffering will again cease to exist and we will be able to eat from the tree of life once more (Revelation 2:7, 21:4; also cf. Romans 8:22-23).

Why is there suffering?

Suffering is a result of the sin of Adam when he disobeyed God. Even death did not exist until that day (Genesis 2:17, 3:19). Once Adam sinned, the curses of sin fell upon mankind and the whole creation descended into a fallen state with death, sickness, sorrow, and pain (Genesis 3:15-19; also cf. Romans 5:12). We now wait for the day when suffering will again cease to exist and we will be able to eat from the tree of life once more (Revelation 2:7, 21:4; also cf. Romans 8:22-23).

Why does God exist?

God exists because he is eternal and has always been (Deuteronomy 33:27; Isaiah 40:28). There is no explanatory reason for this because there is no other greater being that exists (Isaiah 45:5)--he always *was* without a reason being relevant. In other words, there is no "why," only a declaration that he was, is, and is to come without need or a reason (Revelation 4:8). The closest speculative answer that man may be able to devise is that God exists so that he can create.

Why do we exist?

One of the most significant passages as to why we exist tells us that all of creation is for God's pleasure (Revelation 4:11; also cf. Proverbs 16:4, Colossians 1:16). It is also further implied that we are part of God's delight (Proverbs 8:30-31). Since we know that God is love (1 John 4:8), it seems probable that love necessitates creation of other intellectual beings created in his image to share that love with.

Are we to truly take the Bible literally all the time or does it exaggerate at times?

There are some passages that are not meant to be taken completely at face value. For example, we find Jesus saying that those who do not hate their family members cannot be his disciple (Luke 14:26), but then we find out in another passage that what he actually means is that we must love him more than we love our family members (Matthew 10:37). In another place, he tells us that if we are slapped on the cheek, to turn the other cheek and offer that to them as well (Matthew 5:39), but then we find Jesus rebuking somebody who slapped him (John 18:22-23). Yet, afterwards Jesus gave up his life to them even though he had the power to stop it. In another place, Jesus tells us if someone takes our tunic, to give them our cloak also (Matthew 5:40), but the apostle Paul would not even allow people to eat if they refused to work (2 Thessalonians 3:10).

There are other types of statements too that are more historical in nature, such as when it says "all the world" but only means a certain area of the world (Luke 2:1; also cf. Mark 1:5). The whole point is that you need to interpret these types of statements in the spirit of what is being taught or said.

Can we really eat anything we desire?

The apostle Paul says that all foods are clean to a Christian (1 Corinthians 8:8) , and Jesus seems to imply that all food is acceptable as well (Matthew 15:11). Even the letter from the Jews concerning the restrictions for the gentiles only mentions the eating of things strangled and the drinking of blood with a implication that foods sacrificed to idols are restricted as well (Acts 15:20). We are specifically told that if we know food has been sacrificed to an idol, we are not to eat it (1 Corinthians 8:9-13; also cf. Revelation 2:14, 20).

Why are there false teachers?

We were warned by the apostle Peter that false teachers would arise led by their own sensuality and greed (2 Peter 2:1-3). Paul also talks about false teachers and even says that many will depart from the faith to follow them because of their own sinful desires (2 Timothy 4:3-4). Even in the early church this was already happening (Revelation 2:14, 20-22). Why these false teachers are accepted is because many people like their deceptive words; their teachings somehow appeal to their earthly senses or desires.

How do we know God exists?

The apostle Paul tells us that the truth of God's existence is evident within us and that the creation itself is a witness that God exists, allowing us to perceive his eternal power and divine nature so that we have no excuse (Romans 1:19-20). We can also know this by the life and resurrection of Jesus Christ that bears witness to God and his power. Because of all the evidence, the Bible declares that anyone who claims there is no God is a fool (Psalm 53:1).

How do we know Jesus was real?

Though many people are under the false assumption that the Bible is almost our exclusive evidence for the existence of Jesus, they are incorrect on this belief. Christians continued to write volumes of works on Jesus and Christianity from the very beginning up until the present day. We have over 10 huge volumes of genuine Christian writings from several dozen different Christians who lived within the first several hundred years after the death of Christ (the *Anti-Nicene Fathers*). After that, there is more and more testimony. There is a consistent flow of writings that only further validates that Jesus was real. From the second century alone we have writing from two of John's disciples (Ignatius and Polycarp), Barnabas, Justin Martyr, and many others.

Jesus is also mentioned by some early secular writers who lived around the time of the first and second centuries, including the Roman historians Cornelius Tacitus (*Annals* XV, 44) and Suetonius (*Life of Claudius* 25.4). There are no serious Christian or secular scholars that doubt Jesus was a real person on the earth.

How did the Bible come into existence?

Though at least the first five books of Moses and the book of Joshua were accepted early in the history of the Jews (Deuteronomy 31:9, 26; Joshua 24:26; 2 Kings 22:8; also cf. 1 Samuel 10:25), the establishment of the much of rest of the Old Testament canon took place over a long period of time. For example, Daniel was reading the book of Jeremiah for guidance while in captivity (Daniel 9:2). According to Jewish tradition, the canon of the Old Testament was officially established around 400 B.C. by Ezra, Nehemiah, some of the prophets, and others that were part of a group called The Great Synagogue.

For the New Testament, the exact documents to be accepted by the church as part of the New Testament canon was established at the council or Carthage in A.D. 387. All documents to be included needed to have apostolic authority as either having been written by an apostle or an associate of an apostle and conform to the standard rule of faith of what was accepted by the church.

Who wrote the Bible?

The Bible consists of 66 books and was written by at least 40 different authors. The first five books of the Old Testament are believed to have been written by Moses and other parts of the Bible were written by King David, Solomon, the sons of Korah, the sons of Asaph, Ethan the Ezrahite, Agur, Lemuel, Ezra, Isaiah, Ezekiel, Jeremiah, Hosea, Amos, Jonah, Micah, Nahum, Zephaniah, Matthew, Mark, Luke, John, Paul, Peter, James, and Jude. Though numerous men wrote the Bible, it was authored by God as the Holy Spirit inspired the men to write it (2 Peter 1:21; also cf. John 14:26).

How old is the Bible?

Though it is believed that the Old Testament started with the first five books (Pentateuch or Torah) written by Moses (Deuteronomy 31:24-26) in approximately 1450 to 1410 B.C., there is some evidence that some of what Moses used for Genesis may have come from existing documents passed on from earlier times. And the book of Job may possibly be older than the Pentateuch. The other Old Testament books were written after the Pentateuch over the centuries leading up to approximately a few centuries before the birth of Christ. The New Testament was all written within the first century of the common era.

How was the Bible written?

Some scholars today believe that much of what was written in Genesis was originally passed on in oral or written tradition which may have then been used by Moses when writing the first five books of the Bible (Deuteronomy 31:24-26). The book of Job, and any earlier documents used by Moses, were probably written with a iron stylus on either lead or stone (Job 19:23-24). We know that the ten commandments were written on stone (Exodus 24:12, 31:18, 32:15-19). Other early methods of writing included clay tablets followed by papyrus and parchment. We do not have the original document of any Bible book so we cannot be certain what method was used. Yet, most surviving biblical manuscripts are on either papyrus or parchment.

Who created God?

God is eternal being and was not created (Deuteronomy 33:27; Isaiah 40:28). There is no other being greater than God that could have created him (Isaiah 45:5). God has always existed and everything else was created by him. The Athanasian Creed identifies God as uncreated, incomprehensible, and eternal, claiming, "The Father is made of none, neither created nor begotten." And Justin Martyr taught that God was unbegotten, unchangeable, eternal, with ineffable glory and form (*1 Apology* 9, 13, 14). Though we as finite beings have a hard time grasping this just as we might when trying to contemplate the boundaries of the space, it simply means that there was never a time when God was not.

Why would God let someone be mentally or physically challenged?

There may be a number of reasons for this that probably differ in each individual case. We find a person in the Bible who was born blind specifically for the purpose to manifest God's power (John 9:2-3). And Paul suffered a "thorn in the flesh" for the sole purpose of keeping him humble (2 Corinthians 12:7). We cannot understand all the ways and/or reasons of God for allowing the things he does (Isaiah 55:8), but the Christian life is one of trust in which we must believe that all things work together for good for those who love God (Romans 8:28).

What is speaking in tongues and how do you know if someone is REALLY doing it?

Speaking in tongues is when the Holy Spirit works through us in a different language than we understand to either praise God and/or prophesize (Acts 2:11, 10:46, 19:6), or to pray (Romans 8:26). Though the Bible does not provide us with any way to know for certain when tongues are genuine, it does let us know how we are to handle tongues in the company of others. Either they will understand what those speaking in tongues are saying (Acts 2:11) or there needs to be an interpreter that can understand them to translate for others present (1 Corinthians 12:10, 30, 14:27). Tongues are a sign to unbelievers and that is why it requires an interpreter to be present so that it does not seem like madness (1 Corinthians 14:22-23, 27).

Does God have a sense of humor?

Though many Christians struggle to show that God has a sense of humor, we must understand that God is concerned with very serious issues that involve the eternal destiny of mankind. Being God, there is nothing funny about what is going on in the universe nor can there be with so many souls at stake. If you could fully comprehend at all times the destruction of millions of souls, you would not be able to laugh or even smile (our ability to do so in the face of all this is a blessing). Just assume you knew one of your children or beloved relatives was going to die tomorrow, could you laugh or even smile? This is not to say that God doesn't have a sense of humor, only that there are more serious issues that prevent its display in most cases. Though we can forget and/or ignore these issues, God does not because of the finality of it all. For God, this is a time to weep, not laugh (Ecclesiastes 3:4). We can assume this will change once all of this is over and we are all in the presence of God on the new earth (Revelation 21:1).

Having said that, we can find some humor in the Bible such as the story about Balaam and the donkey (Numbers 22:21-29). And some of these passages below, though serious in nature, are also humorous in the way they were written:

> [It is] better to dwell in the wilderness, than with a contentious and an angry woman. (Proverbs 21:19)

> He that blesseth his friend with a loud voice, rising early in the morning, it shall be counted a curse to him. (Proverbs 27:14)
>
> A continual dropping in a very rainy day and a contentious woman are alike. Whosoever hideth her hideth the wind, and the ointment of his right hand, [which] bewrayeth [itself]. (Proverbs 27:15-16)

What does it mean when it says Jesus was half God and half man? Why couldn't he be all God?

Actually, it does not say Jesus was half man and half God. The Bible actually teaches that Jesus is fully God and fully man (John 1:14; Colossian 2:9; Philippians 2:5-8; Hebrews 2:17, 4:15). In order for Jesus to pay the penalty for the sins of mankind and deliver them from the fall brought by Adam, he had to become fully man to redeem the world by living a sinless life and then taking the penalty for the sin of others (Romans 5:14-19). Jesus is called the "last Adam" (1 Corinthians 15:45).

What is the Trinity?

The Trinity is a word termed by Christians to describe God as one being in three persons of Father, Son, and Holy Spirit (Matthew 28:19; also cf. John 15:26, 1 Peter 1:2). Though we are only one being with one center of consciousness from which we experience reality, God is one being and one God with three centers of consciousness which we call "persons." The Father is God, Jesus is God, and the Holy Spirit is God.

What does the Holy Spirit do?

The Holy Spirit was instrumental in the creation of the universe (Genesis 1:20) and the revelation and inspiration of God (John 16:12-15; Ephesians 3:5; 2 Peter 1:21). He also plays a part in the salvation of mankind (John 3:5-6; Titus 3:5; 1 Peter 1:2) and convicts the world of sin (John 16:8-11). He was sent to the earth after the departure of Jesus to indwell us, seal us, and provide help and support (John 14:16-18; 1 Corinthians 6:19; Ephesians 4:30) and to empower us to live a godly life (Galatians 5:16). He distributes spiritual gifts to Christians (1 Corinthians 12:4-11). The Spirit bears witness with our Spirit that we are children of God (Romans 8:16).

Why aren't there prophets today like there were in the Old Testament?

There is no longer a need of prophets since Jesus has now come and everything anyone needs to know for salvation has been revealed. And the Bible says that Moses and the prophets which had already come before Jesus were enough (Luke 16:31). Even after this, God allowed the disciples to perform signs and wonders to validate their testimony about Jesus (Acts 14:3; Hebrews 2:4). After the Old Testament prophets and the validation of Jesus with the miracles, signs, and written testimony of the apostles, there is no further need of prophets like there once was in the Old Testament. This is most likely the meaning of the passage in Isaiah that speaks of binding up the law and the testimony among his disciples (Isaiah 8:16).

Would God really send a really good person to hell? What kind of God is that!

Though it may appear that people are good, Jesus said that nobody is good but God (Luke 18:19). And the apostle Paul tells us that all have fallen short of being good (Romans 3:23). People go to hell because they sin, but Jesus came to offer a way for everyone to be saved. If somebody refuses to accept Jesus when they hear the truth it is because their deeds are evil and they don't want to follow God (John 3:20). Anyone who really wants to follow God will know that Jesus is their Savior and will come to him (John 6:45, 7:16-17).

Where did idol worship come from?

After the fall of Adam, as the population of the world began to grow, men began to turn away from God and go their own way. Because of this they became ignorant of God and instead began to develop their own gods, making idols of animals and other things to worship (Romans 1:21-25). It is also highly probable that the fallen angels who came to earth may have been influential in this activity (Genesis 6:1-5).

Will Buddha Go to Heaven?

How did so many other religions come into existence from two people?

As men began to multiply on the earth, different views began to develop as they abandoned God. Paul tells us that though men knew God, they were not thankful and instead "became vain in their imaginations, and their foolish heart was darkened," which resulted in the worship or idols and false gods (Romans 1:21-25).

This foolish condition of mankind has continued and various religions are constantly created to meet the needs and desires of men who have no desire to seek out the truth and really understand God for who he really is. Today, we have a variety of these types of man-made religions. We are told that the reason men do not come to the truth is because they want to continue in their sins (John 3:19) and that Satan has blinded their eyes (2 Corinthians 4:4).

All the other religions in the world know Jesus existed, but why is he just a great teacher and why is their religion always the supreme?

Because of the revolutionary teachings of Jesus in which he preaches for people to sacrifice self and love others, including their enemies (Luke 6:27), combined with Christianity being the number one religion in the world, it would be difficult for any religion to deny his relevance. Since accepting all of Christ's teaching would make their own religion insignificant and unnecessary, they compromise by concluding he was a good man, teacher, and/or prophet, and often discount Christian claims of what he really taught and said. Even Mohammed is reported to have identified Jesus as a prophet in the Quran (Surah 19:30).

Are Mormons and Jehovah Witnesses Christians?

Though both of these groups are often classified as Christians in the world's understanding of Christianity, neither of them are classified as Christians when based on the biblical account of what a Christian is. Part of being a Christian requires that one is really following Jesus as his Lord and Savior (Matthew 16:24), honoring him in the same manner as one honors God the Father (John 5:23), and believing that he is who he says he is, including the belief that he is eternal God (John 8:24-25; also cf. Isaiah 9:6). Neither Mormons nor Jehovah Witnesses honor Jesus in the same manner as the Father and neither believe that Jesus is *eternal* God. For Jehovah Witnesses, Jesus is the first created being in the universe and is also Michael the Archangel, while Mormons believe Jesus is simply the begotten son of the Father (who was also once a man like us) and the brother of Lucifer.

Why are there so many sects of Christianity? (i.e. Methodist, Baptist, Lutheran, etc)

These different sects are usually a result of division over non-essential beliefs such as the method and necessity of baptism, the nature of man and free will, the significance of sacraments, and other issues. You can already see these types of insignificant divisions taking place in the apostle Paul's day and age (1 Corinthians 1:12-13, 3:4-5). Though there are a number of different denominations, the majority of them still recognize members of other denominations as Christians.

Are Catholics Christian?

All Catholics who have a personal relationship with Jesus Christ are Christians just as all Protestants who have a personal relationship with Jesus are Christians. Those who do not have that personal relationship are not. Though the Catholic Church teaches some false doctrines, they still believe in the same Jesus Christ as Protestants. They believe in Jesus as God, the Holy Trinity, and the necessity of the sacrifice of Jesus on the cross for salvation. They recognize Jesus as their Lord and Savior. The Bible identifies Christians as those who believe in the real Jesus Christ (Romans 10:9). The apparent confusion among some Catholics about certain issues does not negate their salvation if they are trusting and believing in the real Jesus.

Will Jews who don't accept Christ go to heaven?

Any Jew who has heard the gospel and rejected it will not be saved unless they can live a perfect life and abide by the whole law without sinning, which the apostle Paul says is not possible (Romans 3:23). Jesus made it clear that Jews who did not believe in him would die in their sins (John 8:21, 24; also cf. John 9:41). But those who believe in Jesus will be saved (Romans 1:16).

Not Your Typical Sunday School Question

Are all Christians really Christians?

Approximately one-third of the world's population are considered to be Christians, including 85% of those in the United States and 99% of those in Mexico. Yet, the real definition of a Christian is not just somebody who believes in Jesus (James 2:19), but somebody who actual has turned from sin and placed their trust in Jesus as their Lord and Savior (Matthew 16:24). The belief and repentance talked about in the Bible comes from the Greek words PISTEUO and METANOEO, respectively. These two words signify trust, commitment, change of mind, and turning away from sin.

Some people in the Bible had multiple wives. Why can't I?

In Old Testament times, the patriarchs sometimes had more than one wife, but many of them did not choose to do so. Abraham only had one wife and didn't marry another until Sarah died (Genesis 25:1) and Isaac only had one wife. Jacob was tricked into marrying Leah when his real love was for Rachel (Genesis 29:25). The kings of Israel were warned about multiplying wives to themselves (Deuteronomy 17:17). We also know that God instituted a social program to ensure widows were taken care of that could have resulted in more than one wife (Deuteronomy 25:5). It seems that this may have been allowed in early times based on social conditions in which it was necessary to quickly build up a population for protection and/or to ensure women were taken care of by somebody that could protect them and feed them.

The original plan of God is for one man and one woman to join together (Genesis 2:24) and the apostle Paul also tells Christians to have one wife (1 Corinthians 7:2). Every passage in the New Testament indicates that this is the ideal for all Christians.

Why are there so many languages spoken in the world?

After the flood when Noah and his sons came out of the Ark, there was only one language spoken. This one language allowed men to unite outside of God and begin building a city and a huge tower to make a name for themselves and consolidate their resources into one location. God then confounded their language so they couldn't understand each other and they stopped building the city, separating from each other and scattering across the earth (Genesis 11:1-9).

What is the correct language to read the Bible in and why do some people think it can only be the King James Version?

The original language of the Bible is Hebrew, Greek, and a small amount of Aramaic. Of course, the best language in which to read the Bible would be the original languages. Yet, since most of us cannot read the original languages, we must select a translation. A translation is only as good as the translators, so most versions have their good points and their bad points. The best type of translation is one that has been worked on by multiple scholars and gets closest to the original meaning of the text rather than translations made by one person or those with loosely paraphrased passages that tend to stray more often from the actual meaning of the original text.

The insistence by some that the Kings James Version (KJV) is God's version and that other versions are the works of the devil is, of course, nonsense. There are problems in every version, including some serious errors in the KJV. For example, the three witnesses in heaven passage in 1 John 5:7-8 of the KJV is a complete fabrication of the original text.

Should Christians be allowed to be wealthy?

It is not money that is the root of all evil, but rather the *love* of money (1 Timothy 6:10). Nevertheless, there are so many warnings about being wealthy and the difficulty one may have in serving God if they are (Matthew 6:24, 13:22; Mark 10:24; 1 Timothy 6:17; James 5:1), that it is most likely not a good idea for many Christians. Jesus set an example by coming into this world without riches. Having said this, being wealthy is not a sin and may be beneficial in doing God's will for those who can be good stewards without being led astray into self gratification.

How much is one supposed to tithe and what happens if you do not?

Though the Israelites were to tithe 10% of whatever they gained in their work (Nehemiah 10:38), this does not seem to be the practice of the early church. The apostle Paul never specifies a certain amount for people to give and seems rather to teach that Christians should only give what they are led to with a sincere heart (2 Corinthians 9:7). And Justin Martyr describes how in the second century it was only "they who are well to do, and willing, give what each thinks fit; and what is collected is deposited with the president, who succors the orphans and widows and those who, through sickness or any other cause, are in want, and those who are in bonds and the strangers sojourning among us, and in a word takes care of all who are in need" (*1 Apology* 67). Tithing today is from the heart as led by the Spirit of God and should never be a burden on those struggling to make ends meet.

Why do Jews not believe in Jesus; wasn't he the person their prophets had been speaking of?

Actually, though the nation of Israel and most of the religious leaders of his day rejected him, many Jews did and still do believe in Jesus. All the apostles and the first 5,000 or more members of the church were Jewish (Acts 4:4); some of the religious leaders also believed in Jesus (John 12:42; Acts 15:5), including Paul who was instructed under Gamaliel, a leading member of the Sanhedrin (Acts 22:3). Today there are large groups of Jewish believers such as Jews for Jesus, and the amount of Jewish believers within the United States alone is estimated to be over 200,000. Believers over the centuries have included many prominent scholars and rabbis. The nation of Israel as a whole will someday acknowledge Jesus (Revelation 11:13; also cf. Matthew 23:39), but not until the fullness of the gentile conversion has been accomplished (Romans 11:25).

Why is Israel the Holy Land?

Israel is the holy land because God designated it as the place where he would place his name (1Kings 11:36; also cf. Isaiah 66:20, Daniel 9:16). It is believed by many Jews and Christians that this may have been the original location of the Garden of Eden. In addition, we notice that Melchizedek was King of Jerusalem (Salem) and that he was a priest of the most high God during the time of Abraham (Genesis 14:18). Jerusalem is also believed to be the center of the world in Jewish tradition (also cf. Ezekiel 5:5).

Why is there so much fighting between the people in the Holy Land?

The fighting in the holy land is initially the cause of Sarah's decision to allow Hagar to mother a child for Abraham, which brought about the birth of Ishmael. God then delivered a prophecy that he would become a great nation (Genesis 16:10, 17:20). This nation includes many of today's Arabs and possibly even Mohammed. God also declared, "And he will be a wild man; his hand [will be] against every man, and every man's hand against him; and he shall dwell in the presence of all his brethren" (Genesis 16:12), which is exactly what is going on today. Other causes are the rise of Islam and the divisions of conflicting sects within Islam, which has resulted in fighting not only among the Israelites but among each other. And today the city of Jerusalem is recognized as the third most holiest site in Islam as well as the center of Judaism, creating additional conflict. The holy land is also the focus of the end times with the Antichrist set to establish his base of power from Jerusalem itself (2 Thessalonians 2:4).

Why don't we perform sacrifices anymore?

The original sacrifices of animals made by the Israelites could never take away sin (Hebrews 10:4), which means that the original animal sacrifices by faith in God were used as a proxy that was actually applied to the ultimate sacrifice of Jesus Christ on the cross (Hebrews 9:22-28). They may have even been established to make the Jews constantly aware of the sacrifice of death that is necessary for sin so that they could fully understand the sacrifice of Jesus when he took the punishment for all sin on the cross (cf. Hebrews 10:1-5).

Is it wrong to kill someone in war?

This proper answer to this question is very complex and depends a lot on the specific war and why it is taking place. Most Christians know that God instructed the Jews to go to war against specific ungodly nations and the Israelites were also able to defend themselves when attacked; though sometimes God told them to surrender when he was punishing them for sin. But today there are a lot of other factors and the circumstances are not quite that simple.

Let us suppose two Christian countries are fighting each other; at first we might suppose this is wrong, but what if one country is trying to invade another? And the Bible specifically tells us to obey our government if it is truly performing its task of punishing evil (Romans 13:1-7). But, on the other hand, we are instructed as Christians to generally be passive, forgiving, and gentle, and are even told not to fight during the reign of the Antichrist (Revelation 13:10). The answer to this question must be based on the specific war and the circumstances of that war.

Are there Aliens from Outer Space?

The Bible does not mention aliens, though some extraterrestrial proponents attempt to find signs of such in the Bible by twisting around passages such as the one in chapter 28 of Ezekiel that describes an appearance of God. Though aliens are possible and would not contradict biblical truth in any significant way, it appears highly unlikely since God does not mention them even though he would have know about their encounters with our world beforehand. Many Christian leaders believe that they are simply demonic manifestations.

Are angels real?

Angels are mentioned so many times in the Bible that it would be foolish to doubt their existence. They were seen by the patriarchs and apostles on numerous occasions in a large variety of circumstances. Angel comes from Hebrew and Greek words meaning "messenger." They are the messengers of God sent forth in the earth to do God's will and provide service to those who follow God (Hebrews 1:4). The good angels fight against the devil and his evil angels (Daniel 10:13; Jude 1:9; Revelation 12:7).

Will Christians who judge others go to heaven?

We are told not to judge others and are cautioned that our method of fairness in judging will be the same measure used to judge us (Matthew 7:1-2; Luke 6:37; Romans 14:13; 1 Corinthians 4:5; James 4:11). But Jesus also says for us to judge righteously with clarity (John 7:24; Matthew 7:5) and we are told to correct other Christians when they are in obvious sin (Matthew 18:15-17; also cf. 1 Corinthians 5:3). The whole biblical message seems to be that we do not have a right to judge others, especially on their intentions, but that we should love other Christians enough to confront them with sincerity of heart when necessary. Unrighteous judging of others is a sin like any other, but it can be forgiven just like other sins.

Are demons real?

The Bible tells us about a lot of situations in which demons possessed people. Though many in secular circles today would describe these as simply mentally disturbed people, this does not satisfy as a valid explanation since these possessed people exhibited a supernatural knowledge of who Jesus and his apostles were (Matthew 8:29-31; Luke 4:34; Acts 19:15). Jesus and his apostles all believed demons were real.

Why would God let a baby have aids?

Sickness, disease, and infirmity are all a direct result of the fall of mankind, and inflict both Christians and unbelievers alike. Even the apostle Paul suffered from what many believe to be problems with his eyes (2 Corinthians 12:7; also cf. Galatians 4:15) and Timothy had stomach problems and other infirmities (1 Timothy 5:23). In addition, if a baby dies, he goes to heaven, which may not be the case if he had lived to adulthood.

Is abortion wrong?

The Bible clearly identifies the embryo in the womb as a human being created by God (Psalm 139:13-16; Job 31:15; also cf. Luke 1:39-41) and exacts the death penalty for anyone who kills that child (Exodus 21:22-25). Attempts by some to discount Exodus 21:22-25 by implying it means miscarriage as translated in the KJV are easily refuted when we understand that the Hebrew word here is YATSA, WHICH MEANS TO GO OUT, COME OUT, OR EXIT, AND IS OFTEN USED IN THE BIBLE FOR BIRTH (Genesis 25:25-26) and has nothing to do with a baby being hurt or killed. The entire passage is in reference to causing a premature birth and the additional penalties for damage or death to the child and the mother in such a case. Nevertheless, early Christian documents from the first century classify abortion as murder (*Didache* 2:2; *The Epistle of Barnabas*, XIX) as did many of the early church fathers.

What happens if someone grew up in a remote region that has never heard of God or Jesus? Will they go to hell?

The one thing that is very clear in the Bible is that there is no other name under heaven by which men might be saved (Acts 4:12; John 14:6). We know that Israelites who followed God before Jesus were saved and that there were others following the true God during the time of Abraham (Genesis 14:18), and Noah's son Shem was still alive for 35 years after Abraham died (Genesis 11:11). It is apparent that these people were saved based on the future work of Jesus Christ. Is this still a possibility for those who have not heard? That is a matter of debate among Christians and it comes down to trust in God as the loving and merciful God we know him to be.

Is Satan actually a fallen angel or just a general name for a demon?

Satan is translated from the Hebrew word *satan* and the Greek word SATANAS, AND BASICALLY MEANS "ADVERSARY." HE IS CLEARLY IDENTIFIED AS THE MAIN ADVERSARY OF MAN IN THE BIBLE AND THE LEADER OF ALL DEMONIC SPIRITS WITH A KINGDOM IN OPPOSITION TO GOD (JOB 1:8; ZECHARIAH 3:2; MATTHEW 4:8-9, 12:26; ACTS 26:18; REVELATION 12:7-8, 20:9). SATAN WAS FORMERLY CALLED LUCIFER AS AN ANGEL AROUND THE THRONE OF GOD, BUT THEN SINNED BY WANTING TO RULE IN GOD'S PLACE AND WAS CAST OUT OF HEAVEN (ISAIAH 14:12-14; EZEKIEL 28:12-17; LUKE 10:18).

Why doesn't God answer my prayers?

There may be several different reasons why prayer is not answered. Though the Bible says that If you pray to God he will give you what you ask for, it also requires that you have faith that he will do so and that what you ask for is also according to God's will (Matthew 21:22; 1 John 5:15). James specifically says that many prayers are not answered because they are prayers that seek to satisfy our lusts (James 4:3). Also, God will not answer the prayer of the wicked (Proverbs 15:29). In addition, sometimes God's will to answer your prayer might not be according to your conditions or timing, but he may give it to you later under the right conditions (cf. Romans 8:28).

The disciples could perform miracles; why can't people do so more today?

God allowed the disciples to perform signs and wonders to validate their testimony about Jesus (Acts 14:3; Hebrews 2:4), which is probably why God allowed Paul to perform special miracles (Acts 19:11). Now that the Bible has been sealed up there is no further need of signs and wonders for validation of the truth. Also, the Bible seems to imply that there is a danger of those who have special treatment or abilities concerning the things of God being more easily lifted up with pride (2 Corinthians 12:7). Having said this, it does not mean that God does not still perform miracles through people. Even Justin Martyr claimed there were still miracles and healings being performed in the second century (*2 Apology* 6; *Dialogue* 35, 85). The performance of miracles seems to require faith (James 1:6), a godly life (James 5:16), and a gift that only some people receive (1 Chronicles 12:28-29).

Jesus said if you have faith you can move a mountain; if I can't move a mountain does that mean I don't have faith?

The teaching was that we could move mountains if we only have the faith the size of a mustard seed (Matthew 17:20). Yet, the implication throughout the scriptures is that most of us simply don't have the necessary faith to do much of anything and even the apostles were consistently chided for their lack of faith (Matthew 6:30, 8:26, 14:31, 16:8). There are only a few men in the Bible besides Jesus that had enough faith to do great miracles like moving a mountain such as when Moses parted the red sea (Exodus 14:16, 21-22) and Joshua brought down the walls of Jericho (Joshua 6:2-5, 20). But even in these two cases, both were based on specific instructions from God, which would have increased their faith. The implication throughout Scripture seems to imply that most humans simply do not have an amount of faith that exceeds the size of a mustard seed.

What is grace and mercy?

Grace in the New Testament comes from the Greek word CHARIS AND MERCY IS TRANSLATED FROM THE GREEK WORD ELEOS. ACCORDING TO THE THEOLOGICAL DICTIONARY OF THE NEW TESTAMENT, GRACE MEANS "good will, loving-kindness, favor" and mercy means " kindness or good will towards the miserable and the afflicted, joined with a desire to help them." The overall meaning of these terms in our relationship with God as Christians means that God has looked favorable upon us with good will and loving kindness in our afflicted condition of being cut off from his presence with a desire to help us be restored into a right relationship with him and live a godly life (Romans 5:15; Ephesians 2:4-5; Hebrews 4:15-16).

Was Jonah really in a whale?

The two Hebrew words used to describe the creature that swallowed Jonah is GADOWL DAG AND MEANS LARGE FISH (JONAH 1:17). THOUGH THE TEXT DOES NOT SPECIFY EXACTLY WHAT THIS CREATURE WAS, IT HAS BEEN SUGGESTED THAT IT WAS EITHER A WHALE OR A LARGE SHARK. EITHER WAY, WE KNOW THAT JESUS BELIEVED IT WAS A REAL STORY AND EVEN USED IT AS A TYPE OF HIS DEATH AND RESURRECTION (MATTHEW 12:39-40).

Will giving away all my possessions make me a better Christian?

There was one man whom Jesus told him that he needed to give away everything he had to follow him (Mark 10:17-25). Yet, that was a specific case in which Jesus had love for the man and knew that his wealth was the one thing keeping him from really following God. Giving away all your wealth will not necessarily make you a better Christian. We are supposed to give only as we are led in our heart by the Holy Spirit (2 Corinthians 9:7).

Why did God make some body parts that have no purpose (e.g., appendix)?

The appendix is no longer considered a useless organ by many doctors and scientists, but instead is now believed to be a safe storage area for good bacteria as well as some other beneficial uses. Many doctors now advise that you do not remove it. Nevertheless, any body parts that may now be useless, may not have been useless before the fall and even before the flood. After the fall, the body took on a sinful nature and become subject to death (Genesis 2:17). In addition, the environment before the flood may have been quite different and it is believed by many Christian teachers that it didn't even rain until after the flood (Genesis 2:5-6). Because we do not know the circumstances and conditions of these ancient times, we cannot assume that a body part had no use even if it is certain that it has no beneficial use now.

Dying to Know What Happens When People Die

Would God really let so many people go to hell?

Yes. But this doesn't mean that he wants them to go there. The Bible tells us that God does not want anyone to perish (2 Peter 3:9; Ezekiel 18:32) and that Jesus came to die for everyone (John 3:16). Hell was not made for man, but for the devil and his angels (Matthew 25:41). It is sin that sends people to hell, and God has provided a means to be forgiven through Jesus Christ. Those who reject that salvation have made their own free choice to go there.

When will the end of the world take place?

The end of the world as we know it will take place after the Christianity has been preached throughout all the world (Matthew 24:14) and the Antichrist has revealed himself and been defeated by the returning Jesus Christ (2 Thessalonians 2:1-12). Then the heavens and earth will be consumed by fire from God (2 Peter 3:12) and there will be a new heaven and a new earth (Revelation 21:1)

Why do we die?

When Adam sinned, a sinful nature fell upon all men with the result that all men will die (Genesis 2:17; 1 Corinthians 15:22). Death is the result of sin and if Adam had not sinned, death would not have come upon the human race (Genesis 3:22). Yet, since we have all descended from Adam, we will all die as well (Hebrew 9:27).

What happens when we die?

The Bible teaches that upon death, the spirit of a Christian departs to be with Jesus (2 Corinthians 5:8). Though Moses was dead and buried, his conscious spirit was seen in the transfiguration (Matthew 17:3) and the thief was told he would be in paradise that day with Christ (Luke 23:43). The Bible is somewhat silent on the fate of the unsaved during the intermediate state between death and the resurrection for judgment, speaking mostly about the final fate in the Lake of Fire after judgment. Though Luke 16 is often referenced as a claim that they will be in a burning hell while they wait for the judgment, this passage is believed by many commentators to be a parable. Even if it is a parable, it still may give some indication of the conditions that the spirits of the unsaved may experience immediately after death.

After the judgment, Christians will live on in eternal bliss in their resurrected bodies while the unsaved will be cast in the Lake of Fire and find themselves in the outer darkness forever cut off from God (Revelation 21:4-8; also cf. Revelation 14:11).

What is the correct way to dispose of a body, burial above/below ground or cremate?

In the Bible, most of the burials recorded appeared to favor burial in the ground or in tombs (Genesis 25:8-10; Genesis 23:1-4; 1 Kings 2:10) and Jesus was buried in a tomb carved into rock in which people could walk into (Matthew 27:60; John 20:6). On the other hand, the destruction of humans by fire was usually due to punishment for sin (Genesis 38:24; Leviticus 20:14, 21:9; Joshua 7:15-25). Sodom and Gomorrah were destroyed by fire and the second death will consist of being cast into the Lake of Fire. It is easy to see how there is now a Christian preference for burial over cremation, but the reality is that there is no command in the Bible either way and it is highly unlikely that God is overly concerned about the method used to dispose of a body after death.

If heaven is so much better, why do we even have to be on earth?

There needed to be a time where men could decide whether or not they wanted to be in heaven with God. To just create us and place us there in heaven would have not allowed for the usage of free will. God wanted to give us a choice. Justin Martyr saw this time on the earth as a trial period in which men are able to exercise free will so that our relationship with God would be something we wanted (*Dialogue with Trypho* 102).

Will dogs, cats, and animals go to heaven?

This question is not answered directly in the Bible, but we do know that there will be animals here on the earth during the millennial reign of Christ (Isaiah 11:6, 65:25). Some believe that there is a distinction of destiny between men and animals upon death based on a passage that may imply this (Ecclesiastes 3:21). Since the Bible is somewhat vague on this subject, we can get some comfort from many passages that say that God will give us the desire of our hearts and that we will not be sad in heaven (Psalms 37:4; 1 Corinthians 2:9; Revelation 21:4).

What will we look like in heaven?

The apostle John says that we do not know what we will look like, but that we will be like God because we will see him as he is (1 John 3:2). We know we will not die anymore and that we will be equal to the angels in heaven (Luke 20:36). The apostle Paul says that we will be changed, that the perishable will become imperishable and mortality will become immortality (1 Corinthians 15:51-57). To sum it up, we will have an imperishable body and will be like God in some way, but as to exactly what we will look like, John says we do not know for sure.

Noah's Ark

Whatever happened to Noah's Ark if it did exist?

We are told in the Bible that the ark rested on the mountains of Ararat (Genesis 8:4). Immediately upon leaving the ark, Noah built an altar and offered a lot of burnt offerings (Genesis 8:20), which probably required a significant amount of wood. Since God commanded them to leave the ark and go out onto the earth to live (Genesis 8:16-19), and Noah was a builder, it is very possible that the ark was dismantled to build homes and other structures.

There is also another possibility: The remains of the ark could still be somewhere in the mountains of Ararat as reported by many people over the centuries up until the present day. Josephus reported that part of the ship was still there in his day (Flavius Josephus, *Antiquities of the Jews*, XX, ii, 2; I, iii, 5 and 6). He also mentions how barbarian histories report people carrying off pieces of the bitumen as amulets to protect against evil. Early Christians also claimed that the remains of the ark were still there, including Theophilus, Epiphanius, Chrysostom, and others.

Were there dinosaurs on the Ark?

It is believed by many that dinosaurs may have actually been from a prior time on the earth related to the gap theory that insists chapter one of Genesis is the original creation and that the second chapter in Genesis begins our creation period. This is based on the how the Hebrew word for "was" in Genesis 1:2 is more accurately translated "became" in addition to other various biblical passages used for support.

It is also possible that some of the creatures we identify as dinosaurs may have existed at the time of the flood and that others may have already become extinct. If that is the case, those which were not extinct would have been on the ark since God had a pair of every type of unclean land vertebrate enter the ark (Genesis 6:19-20). The book of Job, which some consider as the oldest book in the Bible, may be speaking about dinosaurs when God talks about Behemoth (Job 40:15-24) and Leviathan (Job 41:1-34).

How did all those animals fit on the Ark?

The specifications given the Bible indicate that the Ark was approximately 510 x 85 x 51 feet with over 2 million cubic feet (Genesis 6:15). The ark was so huge, that it took Noah almost 100 years to build it. When calculated, the size of the ark would have allowed for well over 32,000 animals, which far exceeds the amount of animals that most experts believe entered the ark.

What good are mosquitoes for and why were they put in the ark?

Mosquitoes provide a source of food for spiders, fish, birds, and other animals, and are a crucial part of the ecosystem. Though some believe that insects were gathered into the ark, this is most likely not the case. The creeping things in Genesis 7:12 is a translation of the Hebrew word SHERETS AND IS ALMOST ALWAYS USED IN THE OLD TESTAMENT OF ANIMALS, NOT INSECTS. AND EVEN THE SURROUNDING TEXT CLARIFIES THAT THESE CREEPING THINGS WERE SOMETHING THAT HAD BOTH FLESH AND THE BREATH OF LIFE (GENESIS 7:12-13). MOSQUITOES AND OTHER INSECTS PROBABLY MADE THEIR OWN WAY ONTO THE ARK WITH THE ANIMALS AND MANY MAY HAVE ALSO SURVIVED ON THE LARGE AMOUNT OF FLOATING DEBRIS AND BODIES THAT MOST CERTAINLY DOTTED THE WATERS.

Whoops, I Sinned Again

Why do we sin when we know we should not?

When Adam sinned and brought about the fall of creation, all of his offspring inherited a sinful nature which gives all men an inclination toward sin (Romans 5:12; also cf. Psalm 51:5). This is further explained by the apostle Paul who describes the struggle of a man who wants to resist sin but sometimes cannot because of the sinful nature (Romans 7:14-23). Possessing a fallen nature, we are tempted by the pleasures of the world, but when we become a Christian, we are given the Holy Spirit to enable us to resist that temptation (Romans 8:4-5; also cf. 1 Corinthians 10:13). Yet, the struggle does not go away completely and Christians can still be led into sin if they allow it (James 1:14-15).

Are all sins forgivable?

All sins but one are forgivable. Jesus clarified this when he said, "All sins shall be forgiven unto the sons of men, and blasphemies wherewith soever they shall blaspheme: But he that shall blaspheme against the Holy Ghost hath never forgiveness, but is in danger of eternal damnation: Because they said, He hath an unclean spirit" (Mark 3:28-30).

This unforgivable sin was something that could easily be witnessed, should not be prayed for, and was still possible to commit when the apostle John was an old man (1 John 5:16). Though some have attempted to explain this as continual unbelief, it is quite apparent from the passage coupled with John's instance not to pray for it that it meant speaking out against the Holy Spirit. Yet, the significance here is that Jesus was God fully manifesting the Spirit of God coupled with a sinless life. They blasphemed the Holy Spirit while he was working through Jesus.

What happens if a Christian does sin when they know they should not?

A Christian who sins willfully can still be forgiven by God (1 John 1:9). After all, Jesus tells us to forgive those who sin against us an unlimited amount of times (Matthew 18:21-22). But just because God forgives us, it does not mean we will escape the consequences of our sin in the here and now (Job 4:8; Galatians 6:7). If we sin, we will suffer the effects of our sin. Yet, we are also warned that those who practice continual sin may not really know Jesus and are in danger of eternal damnation (1 Corinthians 6:9; 2 Corinthians 13:5; Revelation 21:8).

Is divorce sin?

God clearly has designed the ideal marriage between a man and a woman to be a permanent union (Matthew 19:6). And God hates divorce (Malachi 2:16). Yet, there is an exception that allows for divorce even though it does not require it. When there has been infidelity in a marriage, Jesus gave permission for divorce (Matthew 5:32, 19:9). During Old Testament times, the adulterer was killed (Leviticus 20:10), which would have ended the marriage vows (Romans 7:22). It seems Jesus has set a new standard about infidelity in New Testament times since the death penalty for adultery is not valid in Christianity (cf. John 8:11). It also opens the door for the choice of forgiveness from the spouse that has been betrayed.

Is it sin to divorce and marry again?

The Bible makes it clear that in most cases divorce is sin and that the one who divorces the other is also responsible for the sin of the divorced spouse except in the case where there has been infidelity (Matthew 19:8-9). There is also another exception in which the apostle Paul implies that one is free to remarry if they have an unbelieving spouse that divorces them after they have become a believer (1 Corinthians 7:15).

Is some sin okay while other sins are not?

There is not any sin that is okay with God and all sin is punishable by death (Romans 6:23). Everyone has sinned and is guilty before God (Romans 3:23). But even if men were able to live a life without sin, one small sin would be enough to result in death.

What constitutes a sin? What is right to some is wrong to others, so what makes a sin and who is right?

Sin is rebellion against God's laws and is defined by the apostle John as lawlessness and/or unrighteousness (1 John 3:4, 5:17; also cf. Deuteronomy 9:7; Joshua 1:8). James tells us, "Therefore to him that knoweth to do good, and doeth [it] not, to him it is sin" (James 4:17). And Paul says that he who does something in which he feels it may be wrong is sinning (Romans 14:23). When it comes to issues of the conscience that are not specified in the Scripture, those who are walking closely with God will be instructed by the Holy Spirit and they will know in their heart if it is wrong for them.

Is swearing sin?

The Bible tells us that the wicked are full of cursing (Psalm 10:7) and James warns Christians about cursing (James 3:9-12). The apostle Paul strictly forbids any cussing or swearing from a Christian (Ephesians 4:29). Even Jesus tells us that it is what comes out of the mouth from the heart is what defiles a man (Luke 6:45). With all these passages, it seems apparent that swearing is sin and should be avoided by Christians.

Is watching a R-rated movie sin?

God did not establish the rating system used by us today. Though the R-rating may give us some indication of the content, it often is not much different than PG-13 movies or even some PG movies, both of which can contain subtle ungodly content or taking God's name in vain even though they are not usually quite as direct as an R-rated movie. The rating should be looked at as a guide, but it is the content that determines whether or not watching a specific movies is a sin. We are instructed by the apostle Paul to be transformed by the renewing of our mind so that we are not conformed to this world any longer (Romans 12:2) and James furthers elaborates by telling us to keep ourselves unspotted from the world (James 1:27). Regardless of the rating, movies that include ungodly content should be avoided by Christians.

Is looking at pornography sin?

Jesus clearly implied that lusting over someone other than your spouse is sin (Matthew 5:28). The apostle Paul speaks out against those who have pleasure in the fornication of others as evil and sinful (Romans 1:29-32). By looking at pornography, not only are we failing to renew our mind and remain unspotted from the world (Romans 12:2; James 1:27), but we are harming others by supporting the porn industry even if we don't spend any money. By looking at porn, we further facilitate the damage of all the men and women being lured into that type of life.

Are stealing and killing really equal sins?

Well, this depends. They are equal in the sense that either one makes you guilty of sin and unable to achieve God's standards of required perfection (Romans 3:23). Yet, they are not equal in the degree of harm, which is apparent from the punishments prescribed for these sins in the Old Testament. If you stole, you would have to restore more than what you stole (Exodus 22:1), but if you murdered, you were put to death (Genesis 9:6).

Is it sin to steal bread for a hungry child?

This would depend on the circumstances and conditions and falls under the classification of Christian ethics. For example, stealing bread for a hungry child when you can work for it or pay for it, would definitely be a sin. Now if you were a Jew hiding in Nazi Germany and had no other way to get food for the child, then that may be a different story. Even David was allowed to take the showbread meant only for priests and feed it to those that were with him because they were hungry (Mark 2:25-26).

If anger is a sin, why are we allowed the emotion?

Though unrighteous anger is sin (James 1:20), anger is not always sin in the Bible. God and Jesus both get angry (Psalm 7:11; Mark 3:5; John 12:13-18) In addition, David got angry (2 Samuel 12), as did the apostles (Galatians 2:11-14). The apostle Paul acknowledges that we can be angry and warns us not to hold onto this anger (Ephesians 4:26). We have a fallen sinful nature because of the sin of our ancestor Adam. With that fallen nature, we have a lot of emotions and desires that can lead to sin such as lust and pride. Unrighteous anger is a result of this fallen nature as well.

If I'm single, why can't I lust after another person if I don't act out on that lust? No harm done, so what's the big deal?

The Bible explicitly says that we are not to covet our neighbor's wife (Exodus 20:17), and Jesus say to lust after a woman is a sin (Matthew 5:28), with the implication that to lust after someone who is not your spouse is sinful. It is not only a violation of that person without their knowledge, but can easily lead to other sins. James warns, "But every man is tempted, when he is drawn away of his own lust, and enticed. Then when lust hath conceived, it bringeth forth sin: and sin, when it is finished, bringeth forth death" (James 1:14-15).

Buying My Way Into Heaven?

Is baptism a requirement to go to heaven?

Though some early Christians like Justin Martyr believed that baptism was necessary for the regeneration leading to salvation (*1 Apology* 61), the Bible seems to indicate otherwise. The thief on the cross was saved even though it is highly unlikely he was ever baptized (Luke 23:43). Yet, having said this, we are instructed to be baptized (Matthew 28:19) and the church considered baptism a necessary part of the Christian faith (Romans 6:4; Ephesians 4:5; Colossians 2:12). It is a sacrament that we are expected to obey.

What happens when a baby or young child dies before they hear about salvation?

Though a child is born with a sinful nature (Psalm 51:5), this has been resolved by the work on the cross of Christ that will result in everyone being resurrected from the dead (1 Corinthians 15:22). We will no longer be cut off from God based on our sinful nature we possessed in the flesh since this was rectified in Christ, but instead we will now be judged on our own sins (Romans 14:10; 2 Corinthians 5:10; Revelation 20:12). Children that cannot willfully sin will be cleansed through the work of Christ on the cross. This is why we never find babies or young children going into the Lake of Fire anywhere in the Bible, but only those who willfully practice sin.

Do you have to work for salvation?

No. Salvation is a free gift of God without basis on any works (Roman 5:15-18). On the other hand, James says that faith without works is dead (James 2:17-26) and Jesus says that only those endure and overcome in their faith to the end will be saved (Matthew 24:13; Revelation 21:7). There are many passages that speak either of the free gift of salvation by faith or the necessity of works. A thorough examination of the Scriptures implies that though works are not required to be saved, they are evidence of that salvation in the life of a Christian. As the apostle Paul says, "Examine yourselves, whether ye be in the faith" (2 Corinthians 13:5).

What happens to those that aren't circumcised?

Circumcision was originally a sign between God and Abraham as a seal of his righteousness through faith (Romans 4:11), but it is not required of Christians (1 Corinthians 7:19). The circumcision of the Christian is an inner circumcision of the heart that is spiritual in nature (Romans 2:29). Because of this, physical circumcision is no longer necessary and has no relevance to the fate of men.

Why was Jesus Baptized?

The baptism of John was one of repentance (Mark 1:4; Acts 19:4) and we see the reluctance of John to baptize Jesus because of this (Mark 3:13). Yet, Jesus said it was to fulfill all righteousness (Mark 3:14). Justin Martyr tells us that though Jesus did not need this baptism, he allowed it for the sake of men to provide proof that he was the Christ and that it marked the beginning of his ministry to mankind (*Dialogue of Trypho* 88).

Why did Jesus have to die; why couldn't God just forgive?

When you really examine the concept of sin, you understand that every sin hurts another human being in some way. Even worshipping an idol hurts other people by possibly influencing them to turn away from the true God and as a result end up in the outer darkness for eternity. To forgive sins at the expense of the human beings who are hurt would not only be unjust, but unfair to all. Because of this, there must be a penalty for sin. Yet, in order to satisfy the need for justice, God took the punishment upon himself in the form of his Son, Jesus Christ (Hebrews 2:17). This way the penalty has been paid and justice prevails for all created beings in the universe.